HOMEMADE BODY BUTTER:

30 Body Butter Recipes for Nourished and Soft Skin Today

Table Of Contents

Introduction

I want to thank you and congratulate you for downloading the book, *Homemade Body Butter: 30 Body Butter Recipes for Nourished and Soft Skin Today*.

This book contains proven steps and strategies on how you can make nourishing and all-natural body butters right at home. Everything you need to know along with what tools you'll need, as well as the different benefits that the ingredients would provide your skin with, is here. Many of these ingredients, as you'll soon learn, can be found in your pantry at this very moment. Sounds good, right?

Here's an inescapable fact: Every single day, our skin is exposed to various chemicals from our environment and from the things we apply on it. This can result to different skin issues and the most common of which is dry skin. Constant hydration is a must if you want to keep it healthy, young-looking, and smooth to the touch. Body butters can accomplish all of those and more. However, the body butters that you can buy from the stores may contain certain chemicals that are not suited for your skin.

Here's the solution - homemade ones that would contain ingredients that you chose yourself. Body butters that are all-natural and organic so they won't adversely affect your skin and worsen the problems further. When it comes to organic ingredients, there's a saying that if you can eat it then it's good for your skin and body. Your homemade butters would certainly fall in step with that.

There are many benefits and uses for body butters which make them a lot better than the regular store-bought lotion. They are not greasy and also contain a lot of nourishing nutrients that your skin needs for both health and protection. Some uses for these body butters include:

- Hand care
- Moisturizing rough skin patches
- Face moisturizer
- Make up remover
- After shave leg balm
- Lip balm
- Alternative massage oil

It's time to bring back your skin's health and youthful glow the all-natural way! Remember, moisturize and protect to a more beautiful skin!

Chapter 1: The Basics

Alright, how does one get started with making body butters for their own use as well as to give away as gifts for friends or perhaps, even ones that can be sold for some extra pocket money? You begin with the right tools. After all, no job gets done right if you don't have the proper equipment for it. The things you need for this is pretty basic, and most can be found in your home. Check out the list below:

1. Storage – For this you would need some glass or plastic jars. You can also use aluminum cases such as the ones that used to contain pastilles. You will need to sanitize these, of course, to make sure that your body butter remains clean.

Sanitation can be done through a process called "boiling water bath," which basically requires you to immerse the jars in water then bringing it to a boil. This should take no more than 15 minutes and should only be done on the day you're actually making the body butters.

2. Scales or measuring spoons – These are pretty self-explanatory. You will need these to properly measure out your ingredients and make sure that you're not going overboard with any of them. Too much or too little of one thing can lead to a body butter that's too soft or too firm to whip.

3. A stand or hand mixer – You will need this for whipping the body butter into its proper consistency. An electric mixer would do the job faster, of course, but a hand-powered one shouldn't be too troublesome if you have the energy and time for it.

4. A DIY double boiler – For this, you just need two pots. One smaller than the other but would fit snugly on top of the larger one. You'll fill the bigger pot halfway with some water before placing the smaller one over it. This neat little contraption would allow you to heat your materials gently without scorching them.

5. Glass bowls – Pyrex or anything that's heatproof would be best for this purpose as your ingredients will certainly be hot.

6. Gloves – As a safety precaution for when you're handling hot objects.

7. Piping bags – These are optional but if you want a mess-free way of getting your body butter into the jars then this would be the best way to do it.

So, there you have it, the basic tools that you will need for this project. A good number of them, you don't have to purchase, and would also allow you to recycle.

Chapter 2: Body Butters with UV Protection

Do you think that sesame oil is meant solely for cooking? Not quite. Much like coconut and olive oil, it also has plenty of other uses and benefits. Among which is its ability properly nourish our skin, leaving it moisturized and glowing. That's not all that it can do, however. It can protect your skin from harmful UV rays whenever you go out, and the best bit? It's all natural so the risk for adverse reactions is very low.

Anti-bacterial Body Butter

Ingredients:

- 2 tablespoons of sesame oil
- ½ cup of coconut oil
- 6 tablespoons of cocoa butter
- 15 drops (or more) of tea tree oil
- Your favorite essential oil to mask the tea tree oil scent

Procedure:

1. In a glass container, melt your cocoa butter over low heat. Use a double boiler for this and make sure it doesn't get too hot, but just enough to melt the solid butter.

2. Once it's melted, remove this from the heat and mix in your sesame and coconut oil. Stir this well.

3. Allow this to solidify either in room temperature or by hastening the process through the use of your freezer.

4. Once it becomes firm and opaque, you can whip it using a mixer for a few minutes. If it doesn't whip well, you can bring it back to the fridge, allowing it to harden once more.

5. Add the tea tree oil before mixing it one last time. Keep this in a sanitized and airtight container. Leaving it in the fridge lengthens its shelf life.

Vanilla Bean Body Butter

Ingredients:

- 1 cup of cocoa butter (raw)

- ⅄ ½ cup of sweet almond oil
- ⅄ ½ cup of sesame oil
- ⅄ 1 vanilla bean

Procedure:

1. Melt your cocoa butter then add the sesame oil. Once mixed properly, remove this from the heat and allow to cool for at least half an hour.

2. Grind your vanilla bean using a food processor.

3. Slowly stir in your almond oil to the cocoa and sesame mixture before adding the vanilla bean bits.

4. Wait for it to partially solidify or place it in the fridge for a half an hour or more if needed.

5. Whip this with your food processor and spoon into a sanitized jar for storage.

Cinnamon Body Butter

Ingredients:

- ⅄ 100 grams of coconut oil
- ⅄ 30 drops of cinnamon oil
- ⅄ 15 drops of sesame oil
- ⅄ 50 grams of Shea butter
- ⅄ 1 cinnamon stick

Procedure:

1. Melt your cocoa and Shea butter together, make sure the heat remains low and that it doesn't get too hot. Slowly stir in your sesame and coconut oils before turning the heat off.

2. Remove this from the heat and allow it to cool for about 20 minutes.

3. Once it's cooled down, add your cinnamon oil before whipping it until the texture becomes fluffy.

4. If it isn't whipping as planned, you can place it in the fridge for another fifteen minutes before trying again.

5. Break small pieces of the cinnamon stick into the mixture before carefully spooning it into a clean container.

Rose Body Butter

Ingredients:

- ↥ 10 drops of sesame oil
- ↥ 10 grams of jojoba oil
- ↥ 60 grams of refined coconut oil
- ↥ 3 grams of cornstarch
- ↥ 1 ml of alkanet infused oil
- ↥ 10 drops of rose essential oil

Procedure:

1. Take a glass bowl and in it, mix all of your oils except for the rose one. Add the cornstarch and heat it over a pan of simmering water or using a double boiler. Wait until everything is mixed together.
2. Allow this to cool at room temp so it can set slowly.
3. Once it's cooled down, add your rose essential oil and whip until it resembles frosting. It needs to be light but firm and fluffy.
4. Spoon it into a sanitized jar. This is best refrigerated.

Lavender Infused Body Butter

Ingredients:

- ↥ Half a tablespoon of olive oil
- ↥ 4 tablespoon of coconut oil
- ↥ 1 tablespoon of sesame oil
- ↥ 2 tablespoon beeswax
- ↥ 1 teaspoon of honey
- ↥ 3 tablespoon of aloe vera gel
- ↥ 2 teaspoon f lanolin

- 10 drops of lavender essential oil
- 1 vitamin e capsule

Procedure:

1. Using a double boiler, heat all your oils together with the honey and beeswax.

2. Using a second double boiler, heat your aloe to melt it. Once done, add your beeswax mixture and stir until it mixes together well.

3. Add in your lanolin and stir again.

4. Once everything has incorporated properly, turn your heat even lower and add your essential oil along with the vitamin e.

5. Let this cool down for half an hour or more depending on the need.

6. Whip it until it becomes smooth.

7. Transfer to a small jar and allow to cool before covering.

Pretty in Pink Body Butter

Ingredients:

- 1 cup of coconut oil
- 1 ½ cup of sesame oil
- 3 drops of pink food dye (gel)
- 10 drops of your favorite essential oil

Procedure:

1. Mix your oils and 1 drop of food dye in a large bowl. If your coconut oil needs to be melted, do melt it first using a double boiler and allow to cool.

2. Once you have those mixed together, use a mixer to combine them until they form a light pink whip. Add 2 more drops of the food dye or more, until you reach the desired pink hue that you want.

3. After everything's been incorporated well, you can add your favorite essential oil. Rose is recommended but for something less floral, you can also try lemon or even vanilla.

4. Spoon your whipped body butter into a sanitized jar and keep at room temperature.

Chapter 3: Healthy Glow and Nourishing Body Butters

Coconut oil is one of those multi-purpose ingredients that's also really good for your body – inside and out. It is non-greasy thus making it one of the best moisturizers and solutions when it comes to flaky, itchy, and dry skin. Adding it to your body butter would not only make it super nourishing, as it comes with many essential nutrients that your skin would simply drink up, but also give it a delicious subtle scent.

Mint Infused Coconut Body Butter

Ingredients:

- 1 tablespoon of mint infused coconut oil
- 2 tablespoons of solid Shea butter
- 1 tablespoon olive oil
- Dried rose petals or fresh rosemary
- 1 ml of vitamin E or 1 capsule
- 7 drops of lime or lavender essential oil

Procedure:

1. Begin by melting your coconut oil and Shea butter using a double boiler.

2. Add in the herbs, though you can skip this step too. If you're adding the rosemary or rose petals, make sure to heat this mixture for 30 minutes. Strain it carefully after and squeeze the oil out from the herbs.

3. Wait until your mixture gets cooler before adding your vitamin E and the essential oils you have chosen.

4. Whip this until it gets fluffy and think. This should take about 5 to 10 minutes. You can let it cool for longer to make the whipping much easier.

5. Transfer it to a sanitized jar and you're done!

Magnesium Body Butter With Coconut Oil

Ingredients:

- Half a cup of magnesium flakes

- 3 tablespoons of boiling water
- ¼ cup of unrefined coconut oil
- 3 tablespoons of Shea butter
- 2 tablespoons of beeswax pastilles

Procedure:

1. In a small container, mix your magnesium flakes and boiling water together. Stir this until it dissolves completely. This will form a thick liquid. Once done, set this aside to cool.

2. Take a mason jar or anything similar and place it in a small pan containing half an inch of water. In the jar, combine your beeswax, coconut oil and Shea butter. Keep your heat on medium.

3. Once melted properly, remove your jar from the pan very carefully as it could be really hot. Let this cool in room temperature. The mixture itself should turn slightly opaque.

4. From there, you would need to use a hand blender or an immersion blender at medium speed to whip it up nice and easy.

5. While blending, slowly add your dissolved magnesium a drop at a time to the mixture. Continue blending until everything gets incorporated properly.

6. Put this in the fridge for about 15 minutes and then re-blend until you get the consistency that you want. Store this in a sanitized container and to keep longer, store it in the fridge.

Coconut Body Butter With Vanilla

Ingredients:

- 6 ounces of coconut oil
- 2 ounces of cocoa butter
- Vanilla essential oil

Procedure:

1. Using a double boiler over low heat, melt your cocoa butter.

2. Once it is melted, add your coconut oil.

3. Melt these together but don't let it boil. Once they've incorporated well, remove it from the heat and pour into a mixing bowl. Refrigerate after.

4. Once it's turned slightly opaque, remove it from the fridge and whip. You can use a stand mixer for this if you have one, it will make the job much easier and quicker.

5. When the mixture becomes creamy, put it back in the fridge for about 5 minutes before whipping it a second time.

6. Once it becomes stiff, like chocolate mousse, add your vanilla essential oil (2 drops should do it) then stir a few times.

7. Spoon this into a sanitized jar and store in a cool place.

White Chocolate Peppermint Body Butter

Ingredients:

- ¼ cup of coconut oil
- ¼ cup of cocoa butter
- 1/8 cup of avocado oil
- 1 teaspoon of red raspberry seed oil
- 10 drops of peppermint essential oil

Procedure:

1. Using a double boiler or a saucepan over low heat, melt your butter with the avocado and coconut oil. Try not to let it get really hot. Just enough warmth to melt and combine your ingredients.

2. Remove this from the heat and allow to cool for at least 5 minutes.

3. Add your raspberry seed oil and move the mix to your freezer or fridge. Allow it to cool until it becomes firm enough to be whipped. This should take at least an hour or so. Even if there's some liquid left, a small amount of it should be fine.

4. Take it out of the fridge and add your essential oil.

5. Whip it for a few minutes until it reaches the desired consistency – firm but not too much. If it doesn't whip well, just return it to fridge and allow to cool for a bit more.

6. Store this in a sanitized and airtight container.

Sweet Citrus Vanilla Body Butter

Ingredients:

- ¼ cup of kokum butter
- 1/8 cup of jojoba or avocado oil
- ¼ cup of coconut oil
- 1 teaspoon of raspberry seed oil
- 10 (or more) drops of sweet orange essential oil
- 25 (or more) drops of vanilla essential oil
- 10 drops of lemon essential oil
- 15 drops tangerine essential oil

Procedure:

1. Using a double boiler over low heat, melt your coconut oil, kokum butter and avocado oil together. Whisk this gently and make sure that it doesn't get too hot, just enough to melt and mix the oils together.

2. Once incorporated well, remove this from the heat and allow it to cool for a few minutes.

3. Add your raspberry seed oil to this and place the pan in the fridge or in the freezer. Allow it to cool until the mixture turns opaque. That means it's firm enough to whip. Half an hour should be enough for this and having some liquid left is totally fine.

4. Remove it from the fridge and add your other essential oils

5. Using a hand mixer or a stand mixer, whip this until it becomes fluffy and light. It might take a few minutes but if it doesn't whip properly, you can bring it back to fridge and let it cool for a few more minutes.

6. Store this in a sanitized, airtight container.

Sacred Frankincense Body Butter

Ingredients:

- ½ cup of virgin coconut oil
- ½ cup of Shea butter
- ½ cup of mango butter

- 1 ounce of cocoa butter
- 30 drops of frankincense essential oil
- 1 teaspoon of vitamin e

Procedure:

1. Using a double boiler, melt your Shea butter, cocoa butter and mango butter together. Mix properly.

2. Once done, transfer this to a heat-safe bowl.

3. Stir in your coconut oil – this should melt from the heat of the mixture alone. Make sure everything is incorporated well.

4. Allow this to cool down. Leave it on the countertop for at least 45 minutes and don't put it in the fridge.

5. Stir in your frankincense and vitamin e.

6. Cover the bowl and refrigerate for at least 40 minutes or until it becomes firm enough.

7. Whip this mixture using a hand mixer until it becomes firm and forms peaks.

8. Once you're satisfied with the consistency, transfer this into one of your sanitized jars and store in a cool area.

Chapter 4: Skin Healing Body Butters

Aloe Vera is an absolute gift when it comes to healing the skin as well as protecting it. It stimulates skin regeneration and because of its nutritional and antioxidant qualities, also helps the skin deal with different problems better. It can treat anything from sunburn and blisters as well as any itchiness caused by dry skin. It is also known to help in treating acne, because of its Gibberellins and Auxin content. These are two hormones that provide it with generous amounts of wound healing and anti-inflammatory properties. It would help eliminate acne and at the same time, reduce scarring. Lastly, it also helps minimize the appearance of stretch marks.

Cooling Coconut and Aloe Body Butter

Ingredients:

- Aloe vera gel (you can buy this at any beauty supply store)

- Coconut Oil

- Essential Oil (peppermint and lavender would be great for this)

Procedure:

1. If your coconut oil isn't solid, keep it in the fridge for at least 15 to 30 minutes so it solidifies. Once done, put this into a mixing bowl and whip for about 5 minutes or more, depending on the consistency. It should be firm but also malleable.

2. To this, add your essential oil (5 drops or more depending on its strength) as well as a teaspoon of your aloe vera gel. Whip this once more and make sure everything is incorporated well.

3. Transfer to your container and keep in a cool area.

Key Lime Body Butter

Ingredients:

- ½ cup of coconut oil

- ½ cup of olive oil

- Aloe vera gel

- Lime and lemon essential oils (20 drops each)

Procedure:

1. Place all of your ingredients in a mixing bowl. If your coconut oil is solid, don't melt it. If it's liquid, refrigerate it for at least 30 minutes until it firms up.

2. Stir the mixture for a few times before taking out the electric mixer and whipping it for at least 5 minutes. You can do it for longer depending on how quickly it reaches the desired consistency. If it doesn't whip well, refrigerate it for 15 more minutes before trying again.

3. Transfer this to one of your containers and keep it in a cool place.

Soothing Body Butter with Aloe

Ingredients:

- 2 tablespoons of coconut oil
- 2 tablespoons of Shea butter
- 3 tablespoons of aloe vera
- 1 teaspoon of vitamin e oil
- 1 tablespoon of almond oil
- 10 drops of your favorite essential oil

Procedure:

1. Melt your Shea butter and coconut using a double boiler. Make sure they're mixed together well before removing from the heat.

2. Let this cool down until it becomes opaque. However, don't let it solidify too much or you'll have a hard time whipping.

3. Add your remaining mixture to this and whip all of it together. You'll know when the consistency is just right. Put some in a spoon and hold it upside down. If it doesn't fall, it's ready to use.

4. Transfer to your jar and store in a cool place.

Shea and Aloe Body Butter

Ingredients:

- ½ oz of beeswax

- 3 oz of grape seed oil
- 1 oz of coconut oil
- 3 oz Shea butter
- 2 oz mango butter
- 2 oz aloe vera gel
- 2 oz distilled water

Procedure:

1. To get started, combine all of your butters and melt them together. Stir gently.

2. Once melted put this into a blender and mix it further, slowly allowing it to cool.

3. Add your distilled water and aloe vera.

4. Whip this mixture until it becomes firmer and starts to form peaks. Add the essential oil you're using and mix everything again, making sure everything is well incorporated.

5. Transfer this to your container and keep cool.

Refreshing Peppermint Body Butter

Ingredients:

- ½ cup of coconut oil
- ½ cup of Shea butter
- 1/8 teaspoon of peppermint oil
- ½ cup of aloe vera gel

Procedure:

1. Mix and melt your Shea butter and coconut oil together over a double boiler. Once done, let this cool down for half an hour or until it turns opaque.

2. Add your peppermint oil to the mixture and stir slowly, making sure it mixes well. Add your aloe vera after.

3. Whip everything together until the consistency becomes light and fluffy. Make sure it is firm and that there are no liquids left.

4. Transfer to a container and keep in a cool place.

Mango Body Butter with Aloe

Ingredients:

- 1 cup of Shea butter
- ½ cup of mango butter
- 2 tablespoons of aloe vera gel
- ½ cup of almond oil
- 15 drops of mango essential oil

Procedure:

1. Take your two butters and melt them using the double boiler over low heat. Make sure it doesn't get too hot.

2. Once completely melted, remove this from the heat and add your almond oil along with the mango essential oil. Stir well.

3. Let this cool down or stick it in the fridge for 15 minutes.

4. If it's firm enough, whisk until you reach a nice whip-cream texture or one that suits your preferences.

5. Transfer to a sanitized jar and store properly.

Chapter 5: Body Butter Bars For Smooth Skin

Body butter bars are really no different from whipped ones, since they are just as moisturizing and nourishing. However, for people looking for something much easier to carry around, these would be a great option. Carry them around at the beach or at work and just rub them on dry patches whenever needed. They can be given as gifts too!

Basic Body Butter Bar

Ingredients:

- ¼ cup of beeswax
- ¼ cup coconut oil
- ¼ cup cocoa butter
- 1 tablespoon almond oil
- 1 tablespoon jojoba oil
- Shallow tin container or heat-safe rubber molds

Procedure:

1. In a microwaveable cup or bowl, heat your cocoa butter and beeswax for about 30 seconds each until both melts. Mix together and add your oils.

2. Pour this into your tin container (or mold) then refrigerate.

3. Let it set and cool down before taking them out of the container/mold.

Green Tea Body Butter Bar

Ingredients:

- 2 oz mango butter
- 2 oz Shea butter
- 2 oz beeswax
- 1 tablespoon of matcha (green tea)

Procedure:

1. Melt all of your butters together using a double boiler. Keep the heat low.

2. Once melted together, remove from heat and stir in your green tea powder. At this point you can also choose to add a tablespoon of coconut oil (optional).

3. Prepare your mold by greasing it with some coconut oil.

4. Transfer your mixture to it and refrigerate, allowing it to form before removing and using.

Oat Body Butter Bar

Ingredients:

- 2 oz Shea butter
- 2 oz cocoa butter
- 1 oz almond butter
- 1 tablespoon oats
- 1 tablespoon olive oil (optional)

Procedure:

1. Melt all of your butters together over low heat, mixing them together well.

2. Once done, remove from the heat and set aside. Allow it to cool for at least 15 to 20 minutes before adding your oats. This is so they don't become too soft.

3. Mix well and add your olive oil.

4. Transfer to a prepared mold and allow it to set.

Cranberry Body Butter Bar

Ingredients:

- 1 tablespoon of frozen and crushed cranberries
- ¼ cup coconut oil
- 1 tablespoon Shea butter

- 1 tablespoon vanilla essential oil

Procedure:

1. In a bowl, mix your Shea butter and coconut oil. Use a mixer if you have one.

2. Add your crushed cranberries and mix well.

3. Place this into a sieve and push through with a plastic spatula. This is so no cranberry pieces get into your butter.

4. Add your essential oil.

5. Transfer into your mold or container and refrigerate for a day or two.

Lavender Infused Body Butter Bar

Ingredients:

- 2 oz beeswax
- 2 oz Shea butter
- 2 oz coconut oil
- 15 drops of lavender essential oil

Procedure:

1. Melt your beeswax, Shea butter and coconut oil together. Mix well then remove from heat.

2. Let it cool for a few minutes then stir in your essential oil. Afterwards, grease your mold or container.

3. Pour the mixture into your mold and allow it dry and set in the fridge.

4. To increase the bar's firmness, just add more beeswax.

Cocoa and Coffee Body Butter Bar

Ingredients:

- 40 g of cocoa butter
- ½ tablespoon of finely grounded coffee
- 5 drops of Vanilla essential oil

- 5g of beeswax

Procedure:

1. Melt your beeswax and cocoa butter together. Stir well and don't let it get too hot.

2. Remove from the heat and add your essential oil and coffee.

3. Mix this well and allow to cool for a bit before transferring to your oiled mold.

4. Refrigerate for a day or two before using.

Vanilla Citrus Body Butter Bar

Ingredients:

- 2 oz of beeswax

- 2 oz of Shea butter

- 5 drops of vanilla essential oil

- 5 drops of citrus essential oil

- Lemon zest

Procedure:

1. Melt the Shea butter and beeswax together. Stir this gently.

2. Set aside for a few minutes before adding the essential oil.

3. Pour into your oiled mold and top with the lemon zest, allowing it to set in the mixture.

4. Refrigerate and store in a cool area.

Chapter 6: Floral Scented Body Butters

Flowers have always been used in cosmetics to add both color and a subtle scent. You too can take advantage of this by infusing some with your body butters. Here's how:

Lilac and Vanilla Body Butter Bar

Ingredients:

- 2 oz of Shea butter
- 1 oz of beeswax
- 5 drops of vanilla essential oil
- Lilac petals

Procedure:

1. Melt your beeswax and Shea butter then set aside.
2. Add your essential oil and lilac petals, stir slowly.
3. Pour this into your oiled mold through a sieve to filter out the petals.
4. Refrigerate.

Lavender and Chamomile Body Butter Bar

Ingredients:

- 3 oz of coconut oil
- 3 oz of jojoba oil
- 2 oz of beeswax
- 5 drops of lavender essential oil
- Chamomile and lavender flower buds

Procedure:

1. Infuse your oils. Mix your oils and beeswax together, melting any clumps before stirring in the flower buds. Don't let this boil but keep stirring for at least 3 minutes.

2. Set aside and pass this mixture through a sieve and into another bowl. Add your essential oil and stir.

3. Transfer to your mold, sprinkle some of the buds into it then refrigerate.

Vanilla and Rose Body Butter Whip

Ingredients:

- ½ cup of cocoa butter
- 2 tablespoons of coconut oil
- 5 drops of vanilla essential oil
- 1 capsule of vitamin e
- Rose petals

Procedure:

1. Mix your cocoa butter and coconut oil over low heat.

2. Once mixed, turn off the heat and allow to cool for a few minutes before adding the petals. Stir for another 2 minutes.

3. Pass this through a sieve and transfer to a bowl. Add your vitamin e and essential oil. Stir well then refrigerate.

4. Once it turns opaque, take it out and whip for at least 5 minutes or until it reaches the consistency you like.

5. Transfer to a sanitized container and store in a cool area.

Jasmine and Coconut Milk Body Butter

Ingredients:

- ½ cup of coconut oil
- ½ cup of Shea butter
- 3 tablespoons of coconut milk
- A teaspoon of aloe vera gel
- 5 drops of Jasmine essential oil

Procedure:

1. Melt your oil and butter over low heat. Mix well.

2. Take the mixture off the heat and add your essential oil and coconut milk. Stir until incorporated. Add your aloe vera gel and stir again.

3. Let this cool off in the fridge for 15 to 30 minutes.

4. Whip until it forms peaks then transfer to your container.

Refreshing Lemon and Chamomile Body Butter Bar

Ingredients:

- ½ cup of beeswax
- ½ cup of Shea butter
- 3 tablespoons of olive oil
- Chamomile essential oil
- Lemon zest

Procedure:

1. Mix your beeswax and butter, let these melt over low heat.

2. Once melted, remove it from the heat and set aside for at least 5 minutes before adding your olive oil and essential oil. Mix well.

3. Transfer this to your mold slowly, adding your lemon zest while you pour.

4. Refrigerate for a day or two before using.

Chocolate and Vanilla Flower Bronzing Body Butter

Ingredients:

- 2 tablespoons of organic cacao powder
- 5 drops of vanilla essential oil
- ½ cup of cacao butter
- ½ cup of coconut oil
- ½ cup of beeswax

Procedure:

1. Melt your coconut oil, cacao butter and beeswax together. Make sure everything is mixed and melted well.

2. Removed this from the heat and add your cacao powder to it. Stir well until it becomes incorporated then add your essential oil.

3. Stir this some more before transferring to your mold.

4. Refrigerate for a couple of days before using.

Conclusion

Thank you again for downloading this book!

I hope this book was able to help you better understand the process of making your own body butter at home as well as the benefits that the different ingredients can provide you with.

The next step is to give the recipes a try! Find out which one works the best for your skin and give some away to your friends and loved ones. Many people have also turned this into a small-scale home business. It all depends on how creative you can get.

Finally, if you enjoyed this book, please take the time to share your thoughts and post a review on Amazon. It'd be greatly appreciated!

Thank you and good luck!